NATIONAL GEOGRAPHIC | GLOBAL ISSUES

STANDARD OF LIVING

Andrew J. Milson, Ph.D.
Content Consultant
University of Texas at Arlington

Acknowledgments

Grateful acknowledgment is given to the authors, artists, photographers, museums, publishers, and agents for permission to reprint copyrighted material. Every effort has been made to secure the appropriate permission. If any omissions have been made or if corrections are required, please contact the Publisher.

Instructional Consultant: Christopher Johnson, Evanston, Illinois

Teacher Reviewer: Patricia Lewis, Humble Middle School, Humble, Texas

Text Credits

12 Excerpt from Spicy Hot Colors by Sherry Shahan. Text copyright ©2004 by Sherry Shanahon. Illustrations ©2004 by Paula Barragan. Reprinted by permission of August House Little Folk. All rights reserved.

Photographic Credits

Cover, Inside Front Cover, Title Page ©Yu Chu Di/ Redlink/Redlink/Corbis. **3** (bg) ©Stockbyte/Getty Images. **4** (bg) ©Paul Hardy/Corbis. **6** (bg) ©Ludovic Maisant/Hemis/Corbis. **8** (bg) Mapping Specialists. **10** (bg) ©Dave G. Houser/Corbis. **13** (bg) ©Ellen B. Senisi/The Image Works. **14** (t) ©Bob Krist/Corbis. **15** (cr) ©Jeffrey Rotman/Corbis. **16** (bg) ©John Moore/Getty Images. **19** (bg) ©John Moore/Getty Images. (tl) ©Syed Jan Sabawoon/epa/Corbis. **20** (bg) ©Maike Albrecht/dpa/Corbis. **22** (bg) ©Aaron Kisner courtesy of Vital Voices Global Partnership/ PR NEWSWIRE/Newscom. **22** (cl) ©Philip Andrews/ National Geographic Society. **25** (bg) ©Philip Andrews/National Geographic Society. **27** (t) ©Jim West/Alamy. **28** (tr) ©Photos and Co/Lifesize/Getty Images. **30** (tr) ©Philip Andrews/National Geographic Society. (br) ©Birgitte Wilms/Minden Pictures. **31** (bg) ©Stockbyte/Getty Images. (tr) ©Ludovic Maisant/Hemis/Corbis. (br) ©Paul Hardy/Corbis. (bl) ©Bob Krist/Corbis.

MetaMetrics® and the MetaMetrics logo and tagline are trademarks of MetaMetrics, Inc., and are registered in the United States and abroad. The trademarks and names of other companies and products mentioned herein are the property of their respective owners. Copyright © 2010 MetaMetrics, Inc. All rights reserved.

For permission to use material from this text or product, submit all requests online at www.cengage.com/permissions.

Further permissions questions can be emailed to permissionrequest@cengage.com.

Visit National Geographic Learning online at www.NGSP.com.

Visit our corporate website at www.cengage.com.

ISBN: 978-0-7362-9764-6

Printed in Mexico
Print Number: 07   Print Year: 2020

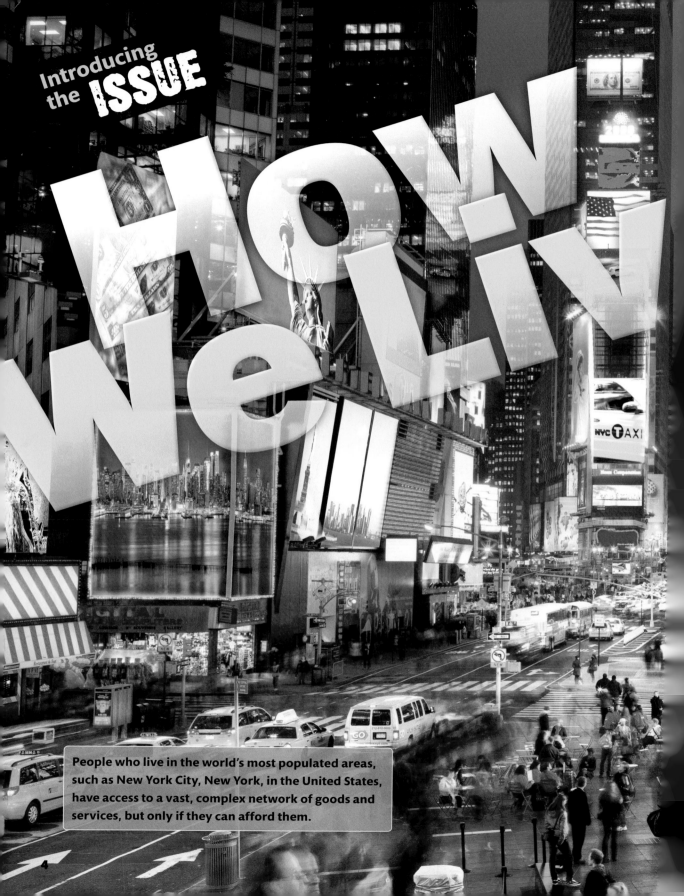

HOW We Liv

People who live in the world's most populated areas, such as New York City, New York, in the United States, have access to a vast, complex network of goods and services, but only if they can afford them.

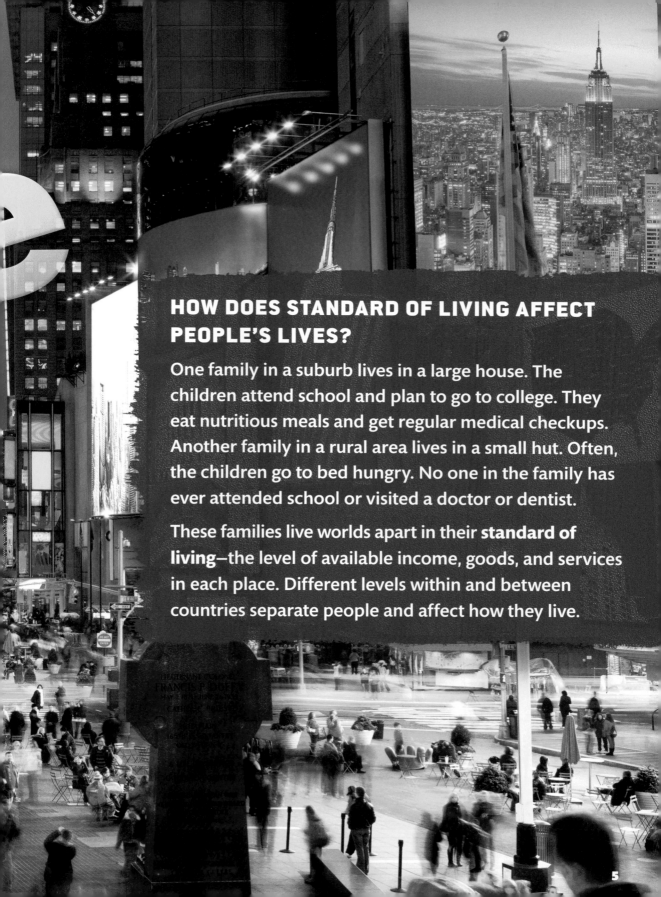

HOW DOES STANDARD OF LIVING AFFECT PEOPLE'S LIVES?

One family in a suburb lives in a large house. The children attend school and plan to go to college. They eat nutritious meals and get regular medical checkups. Another family in a rural area lives in a small hut. Often, the children go to bed hungry. No one in the family has ever attended school or visited a doctor or dentist.

These families live worlds apart in their **standard of living**—the level of available income, goods, and services in each place. Different levels within and between countries separate people and affect how they live.

People living below the poverty line would not be able to afford even simple luxuries, such as buying flowers at a popular London street market.

WHAT IS STANDARD OF LIVING?

To measure standard of living, economists look at whether people can afford the basics: clean water, food, shelter, and clothing. Depending on where they live, some people can barely meet their needs while others enjoy luxuries.

Affording the basics depends largely on **income**, which is the amount of money a person makes in a certain period of time. A low-wage earner in one country might be a high-wage earner in another because **cost of living** varies from place to place. Cost of living is the amount of money required to maintain a certain standard of living.

Other factors that determine standard of living include access to education and health care. Level of education influences a person's income. Access to health care affects **life expectancy**, which is the number of years that a person in a particular group or place can expect to live. People with higher standards of living generally live longer lives.

COMPARING STANDARDS OF LIVING

One way to compare standards of living among countries is to look at the number of people living below the poverty line. The **poverty line** is the minimum income required to meet basic needs. The poverty line for a family of four in the United States in 2010 was $22,314. About 15 percent of Americans lived below the poverty line in 2010, compared to 65 percent in Honduras and less than 2 percent in Taiwan.

What do these kinds of statistics say about people's lives? The simplest answer is that most people can meet their basic needs in wealthier countries but not in poorer countries. Next, you'll read about two countries—Costa Rica and Afghanistan—with different standards of living and learn how the differences affect people's lives.

COUNTRIES WITH THE HIGHEST STANDARD OF LIVING

1 NORWAY
2 AUSTRALIA
3 NETHERLANDS
4 UNITED STATES
5 NEW ZEALAND
6 CANADA
7 IRELAND
8 LIECHTENSTEIN
9 GERMANY
10 SWEDEN

Source: United Nations HDI 2011 Rankings

Explore the Issue

1. **Summarize** How is standard of living measured?

2. **Analyze Effects** How does standard of living affect people's lives?

Value of all goods produced in a year, divided by a country's population (U.S. Dollars, 2010)

- more than 40,000
- 20,000–39,999
- 10,000–19,999
- 5,000–9,999
- less than 5,000
- no data

NORTH ATLANTIC OCEAN

NORTH AMERICA

ALBANIA Many people live in rural poverty, making Albania one of Europe's poorest countries.

NORTH ATLANTIC OCEAN

UNITED STATES Natural resources, a stable political system, and an educated workforce have helped most U.S. citizens achieve a high standard of living.

CASE STUDY 1

COSTA RICA A high literacy rate, quality health care, and natural resources help to make Costa Rica "the happiest nation on earth."

SOUTH AMERICA

SOUTH PACIFIC OCEAN

SOUTH ATLANTIC OCEAN

Explore the Issue

1. **Interpret Maps** What are two continents with countries that produce less than $5,000 per year per person?

2. **Analyze Causes** What are some factors that contribute to a low standard of living?

nd the World

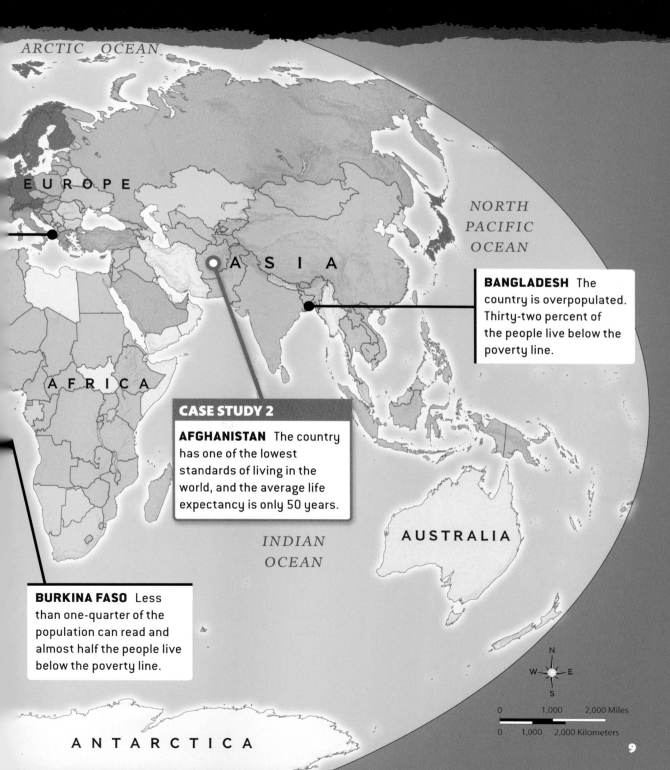

ARCTIC OCEAN

EUROPE

ASIA

NORTH PACIFIC OCEAN

AFRICA

BANGLADESH The country is overpopulated. Thirty-two percent of the people live below the poverty line.

CASE STUDY 2

AFGHANISTAN The country has one of the lowest standards of living in the world, and the average life expectancy is only 50 years.

INDIAN OCEAN

AUSTRALIA

BURKINA FASO Less than one-quarter of the population can read and almost half the people live below the poverty line.

N
W E
S

0   1,000   2,000 Miles

0   1,000   2,000 Kilometers

ANTARCTICA

Living Well in
COSTA RI

At the entrance to San Rafael Church in
Zarcero, Costa Rica, visitors find shade
under an archway of living sculptures.

THE RICH COAST

As a boy, Rember Guevara (gay-BAH-rah) and his family fled El Salvador, which was in the middle of a civil war, and moved to Costa Rica. Guevara's parents enrolled him in school, where he started four grades below other children his age. In high school, he was elected class president. As an adult, he now owns a growing car rental agency in Costa Rica. Like most other Costa Ricans, Guevara lives simply but comfortably.

Costa Rica—which means "the rich coast"—has one of the highest standards of living in Central America. The majority of people live simply by American standards, but they can comfortably meet their needs. Public education is free through high school, and the **literacy rate**—the percentage of people who can read and write—is 95 percent. About 24 percent of the people live below the poverty line, as compared to 15 percent of the people who live in the United States. The life expectancy rate—75 years for men and 81 years for women—is very close to that of the United States, 76 years for men and 81 years for women.

EDUCATION INSTEAD OF WAR

How has Costa Rica managed to prosper in a region where many of its neighbors live in poverty? The country's history of political stability is one reason its people enjoy a higher standard of living.

Costa Rica has another important advantage over its Central American neighbors. It has a more educated workforce. The country instituted free public education in the 1800s. Today, almost one-fourth of government spending goes to education. Costa Ricans value education and proudly state, "We have more teachers than soldiers." It's customary for families to hang framed school diplomas in their homes. While Costa Rica has a literacy rate of about 95 percent, the rate of neighboring countries is much lower: Guatemala is 69 percent and Nicaragua is 68 percent.

PERCENTAGE OF POPULATION LIVING BELOW POVERTY LINE IN CENTRAL AMERICA

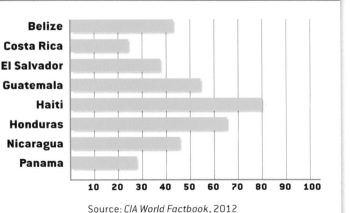

Source: *CIA World Factbook*, 2012

MIXING THINGS UP

Another reason for the high standard of living in Costa Rica is that the country has begun to diversify its economy. A **diversified economy** is one that produces a variety of products and services, not just one or two. Costa Rica's economy once depended almost entirely on agriculture. Bananas were the country's most important export crop. It is risky for a country to depend on only one type of economic activity. If that activity declines, people have nowhere to turn for jobs.

Costa Rica has been working hard to diversify its economy. Service industries such as real estate, insurance, transportation, and telecommunications now play an important role in the Costa Rican economy. In addition, manufacturing of products such as textiles, microprocessors, and medicines has grown.

NATURAL BEAUTY AND TOURISM

One economic activity—tourism—has been most responsible for the country's success. Beautiful mountains and beaches attract tourists. Rain forests offer incredible **biodiversity**— or great variety of plants and animals. These forests are home to 850 species of birds, including colorful macaws and toucans. As far as plant life, the country boasts 1,000 species of orchids alone. In addition, Costa Rica's reputation as a safe, stable country makes it attractive to travelers. So Costa Rica has developed **ecotourism** into a booming industry. Ecotourism is travel to support a region's wildlife ecology and conservation efforts.

When tourists come to Costa Rica, hotels, restaurants, and rental car companies, such as the one owned by Rember Guevara, benefit from their spending. Since the 1990s, tourism has become the most important source of revenue in Costa Rica.

The University of Costa Rica has a main campus near San José, with other campuses around the country. The university offers study-abroad programs in tropical conservation and other subjects. Each year, Costa Rica's programs attract students from all over the world. They pay tuition to participate in the programs and to stay with host families, all of which brings income to Costa Ricans.

Costa Rican students study in their classroom. These students will begin college at age 15. Over 95 percent of college-age students are literate.

A hiker crosses a hanging bridge in the rain forest near Arenal Volcano in Costa Rica. Tourists come from all over the world to experience the country's unique natural resources.

HEALTH, NOT WEAPONS

Besides investing in education and conservation, Costa Rica invests in health care for its people. One reason Costa Rica can afford to invest in public health care is that it supports no regular military.

Because most health facilities are located in its cities, Costa Rica brings health care to rural people. Medical personnel regularly visit the outreach clinics, which are staffed by medical assistants. The rural health program also educates people on health topics, such as nutrition and immunization. The results of the country's strong public health program can be seen in its high life expectancy rates.

Because the country offers high-quality, affordable health care and excellent medical facilities, people from other countries travel there for medical treatment. As a result, medical tourism is growing. For example, many Americans and Canadians who come for medical treatment often extend their trips to enjoy the Caribbean climate and the region's biodiversity.

A HAPPY PLACE TO LIVE

Costa Rica may not be a perfect paradise with the highest standard of living in the world, but its people seem generally healthy and happy. In fact, one American columnist labeled it "the happiest nation on earth," based on how it ranked in several studies of happiness. One study evaluated self-reported happiness, life expectancy, and the people's impact on the environment. Tiny Costa Rica tops the list! As the country shapes its future, good management of its natural resources should remain a top priority.

The researcher above uses a submersible—a small underwater craft—to photograph the variety of marine life found in the waters of Cocos Island National Park. Costa Rica's conservation efforts protect critically endangered species in this large marine reserve.

Explore the Issue

1. **Analyze Causes** What factors contribute to Costa Rica's high standard of living?

2. **Summarize** How has Costa Rica improved its economy?

SURVIVING IN WAR-TORN AFGHANIST

Life goes on, as this photograph shows. Afghans walk near a new hotel built amidst the ruins of war in Kabul, Afghanistan.

RETURNING HOME

In 2002, while his California schoolmates took a class trip, 17-year-old Said Hyder Akbar (suh-EED HIH-duhr AHKH-bahd) did something few Americans would dream of doing. He visited war-torn Afghanistan, his family's homeland. The new Afghan president had asked Akbar's father to return and help rebuild the country, so Akbar went along. While there, he translated for American forces, visited a battle zone, and survived a surprise attack. After attending college at Yale, Akbar wrote a book about his experiences, called *Come Back to Afghanistan*. He then returned to Afghanistan.

Millions of Afghans, like Akbar, returned to their country after an Islamic governing group called the Taliban was overthrown in 2001. The returning Afghans came mostly from neighboring countries, where they had lived in refugee camps. The returning refugees raised the country's population by some 25 percent. Their life in Afghanistan was far from easy, however.

THE DEADLY COST OF WAR

War has raged in Afghanistan since the late 1970s. The Russians fought there for 9 years, and American forces have fought the Taliban there for more than 10 years. Before and during occupation, Afghans have fought one another in civil wars. Today, few people earn a decent living. For most, it's a day-to-day struggle just to survive.

War and political instability have made Afghanistan one of the world's poorest countries. About 36 percent of the people live below the poverty line of $1 a day, and many more live just barely above the poverty line. In the United Nations' ranking of countries by standard of living, Afghanistan falls to number 172 out of 187 countries in the world.

Warfare and years of oppressive government have produced a country where most of the people cannot read and write. The literacy rate in Afghanistan is 28 percent. Boys and young men have fought in the wars rather than getting an education. Girls were not allowed to attend school while the Taliban ruled the country. Members of this group follow an extreme form of Islam, in which girls and women are not permitted to work or be educated.

A DANGEROUS AND DIFFICULT LIFE

As a result of these factors, life for most Afghans is extremely difficult. Decades of warfare have destroyed or damaged homes, public buildings, power plants, and roads, and many people lack access to clean water and electricity. Every region of the country is riddled with land mines, and more than 75 percent of those killed by such explosive devices in 2011 were children.

Many workers in Afghanistan are unskilled, and the unemployment rate is about 35 percent. Almost 80 percent of the people depend on agriculture or related businesses for employment. In rural areas, farmers attempt to earn a living on dry land with primitive irrigation. Among the poorest rural people are the widows and their children. About 50 percent of children up to 5 years of age suffer from **malnutrition**, a lack of the right amount of nutrients needed to maintain a healthy body.

INADEQUATE HEALTH CARE

The lack of sanitation and reliable power makes it hard for people to lead healthy lives. Without access to clean water, people are more prone to disease. Water-borne and food-borne diseases are common in Afghanistan, and the risk of contracting them is very high.

A low standard of living affects health in other ways too. When people cannot afford nutritious food, they often develop a variety of health problems. But Afghanistan does not have enough doctors to treat the sick; the country has only 1 doctor for every 5,000 people. In contrast, the United States has about 13 doctors for every 5,000 people. Afghanistan's life expectancy rate of 50 years is among the lowest in the world.

Afghanistan dramatically illustrates the connection between a low standard of living and health problems. Besides a low life expectancy rate, it has the second highest **infant mortality rate** in the world. The infant mortality rate is the number of infant deaths per 1,000 live births. In Afghanistan, about 122 infants die for every 1,000 live births. The rate is the highest in the world. In sharp contrast, this number is 6 in the United States.

Afghan trading families lead a difficult life, one that keeps them from attaining a higher standard of living.

Vehicles, vendors, and pedestrians fill Kabul's city center. Poor roads and conflicts make travel outside of the city dangerous.

In spite of the enormous challenges that come with living in a country scarred by decades of war, these Afghan textile traders look forward to a brighter, more prosperous future.

MEETING PRESENT CHALLENGES

Afghanistan faces huge challenges to rebuild and raise its standard of living. Providing education is one important step. The country's constitution adopted in 2004 makes education a right of all citizens. Unfortunately, many schools have been destroyed, and those that remain lack adequate space and supplies. International aid is needed to improve the situation.

Afghan-American Khaled Hosseini (KAL-ihd hoh-SAY-nee) is one person who is trying to help. A doctor and the author of two best-selling novels about Afghanistan, Hosseini has set up a charity to provide funds for Afghan schools and award college scholarships to Afghan students. The charity is helping to improve Afghanistan's standard of living in other ways as well. It has given money to build shelters for 1,000 people without homes and has distributed seeds and fertilizer to Afghan farmers.

REBUILDING FOR TOMORROW

An Afghan woman named Kamila Sidiqi (kuh-MEE-lah suh-DEE-kee) not only has survived war in Afghanistan, but she also has helped others. When her father and older brother fled the country, Sidiqi needed to provide for her younger siblings. Under Taliban rule, women were forbidden to work outside the home. So she and her sisters began a dressmaking business in their home and sold clothing to local storeowners. The business grew so much that Sidiqi hired girls from the neighborhood. She now teaches other women how to run businesses.

Small businesses, such as Sadiqi's, improve the economy. Customers buy goods from people they know and trust. In turn, shopkeepers invest in the community. Through education and determination, progress is slowly gaining ground in Afghanistan. With the help of peace-keeping forces from other countries, Afghans can begin to rebuild and secure a brighter future.

Explore the Issue

1. **Find Main Ideas** What is the major reason for the low standard of living in Afghanistan?

2. **Identify Solutions** What role does education play in raising the standard of living of all Afghans?

Providing Education Opportunities

Maasai children eagerly gather around teacher
Kakenya Ntaiya to hear a humorous story.

EDUCATION FOR ALL

The Maasai (mah-SY) of East Africa have lived as nomads raising herds of cattle for hundreds of years, but the land can no longer adequately support their population. To help raise the Maasai's standard of living, which is low, the government of Kenya has encouraged them to settle in villages and on farms. Yet that step alone is not enough to lift them out of poverty.

One reason is lack of education. Although Kenya requires all children to attend school for at least eight years, many Maasai families take their daughters out of school at age 13 so they can marry. Traditionally, the Maasai have not encouraged girls or women to continue their education. A determined young Maasai girl, Kakenya Ntaiya (kah-KEN-yuh nuh-tuh-EE-yuh), challenged this practice. Ntaiya, who today is a National Geographic Emerging Explorer, has taken extraordinary steps to improve education for girls in Kenya.

In developing countries, educating women tends to raise the people's standard of living. Educated women often have fewer children, which reduces overpopulation. **Overpopulation** is the condition of having more people than an area can support. It is one of the numerous reasons for low standards of living in many of the developing countries around the world.

A YOUNG GIRL'S DREAM

Born in a small Kenyan village, Ntaiya was the first of eight children. Her father worked in a distant city, and her mother labored in sugarcane fields. As the oldest child in the family, Ntaiya had to help with all the chores, work in the fields, and care for her siblings.

When she turned five, her parents announced her engagement to a village boy. This was the custom among traditional people in Kenya. But Ntaiya dreamed of becoming a teacher, so she negotiated with her parents to be allowed to attend high school. In exchange for their permission, she told her parents that she would follow Maasai customs and study hard to earn good grades. True to her promise, Ntaiya achieved high grades and won a college scholarship to study in the United States. She looked forward to this exciting opportunity.

KEEPING A PROMISE

As Ntaiya prepared for college, her father became ill and could not work. Her family had no money to send Ntaiya overseas. Again she negotiated, this time with a village leader. She promised to use her education to help her people. The village worked hard to raise the money to send her to college, and Ntaiya kept her promise.

Ntaiya attended graduate school to earn an advanced degree in education. She also worked to achieve an ambitious plan—to build a girls' school in her village. In 2009, she opened the Academy for Girls, the first primary school for girls in that part of Kenya.

"I'm helping girls who cannot speak for themselves," Ntaiya explains. "Why should they go through the hardships I endured? They'll be stepping on my shoulders to move up the ladder—they're not going to start on the bottom."

In its first two years, the Academy enrolled 60 students. Ntaiya's goal is 150 students in grades four through eight. "We keep class sizes very small, so each girl receives a great deal of individual attention," Ntaiya says.

MAKE A DIFFERENCE

Kakenya Ntaiya raises money for her school by accepting invitations to speak with helping organizations all over the world. On her trips abroad, she shares the story of one girl's promise to her people. Because Ntaiya believes that education will empower the girls and their families, she is helping the Maasai shape a brighter future for themselves.

Kakenya Ntaiya succeeds because she set goals and works hard to achieve them. You, too, can set worthwhile goals and use your skills to make a difference in your world. The activity on the next two pages gives you a way to start.

Explore the Issue

1. **Draw Conclusions** Why is it important to educate Maasai girls beyond elementary school?

2. **Make Predictions** How might the work of Kakenya Ntaiya affect the standard of living of her people?

Kakenya Ntaiya shares a new book with Maasai children who are learning to read.

Organize
a Food Drive
—and report your results

People in need are everywhere, not just in poor countries. Most communities have one or more food banks, places that collect and distribute food to people in need. Organize a food drive in your school, and donate the food to a community food bank. You'll be sharing food with people who really need it.

RESEARCH

- Find out the name, location, and phone number of a food bank in your community.

- Call the food bank to find out what kinds of food items they collect and to ask about their hours of operation.

- Make a list of the types of food you plan to collect. Be sure to include locally grown produce and products.

ORGANIZE

- Prepare a flyer announcing your food drive. Indicate the date that you want students to bring their donations to school.

- Make copies of the flyers, and distribute them to the students and teachers at your school.

- Obtain large boxes, label them, and place them in each classroom before the day of the food drive.

Community volunteers make a difference by serving meals to those in need.

DELIVER

- Collect all the boxes of donated food.

- Ask volunteers to help inventory and organize the food into bags and boxes that can be carried efficiently.

- Call the food bank and arrange the best time to deliver the food.

- Line up volunteers and adults at school to help load and transport the donated food to the food bank.

SHARE

- Announce the results of your food drive on your school's intercom, telling how many boxes of food you collected.

- Write a letter to your community newspaper, describing your efforts and encouraging others to donate to the food bank.

- Interview the director of the food bank to ask about the number of people the food bank serves. Share the information by giving talks to other classes at your school.

Write an Argumentative Article

What action would you like to see people take to improve the standard of living in the United States? Promote bicycling to improve our health? Increase the number of teacher aides to give individual attention to students who need help? Your task is to identify a way to improve our standard of living and to write a convincing argument promoting your claim.

RESEARCH

Use the Internet, books, and articles to find the following information:

- Data on the standard of living in the United States
- Suggested actions to improve the standard of living
- Evidence to support these suggestions

As you do your research, be sure to take good notes and document your sources.

DRAFT

Review your notes and identify a course of action that you will recommend to others. It may be one you've researched, or it may be your own idea. Then write a draft.

- The first paragraph, or introduction, should get the reader's attention. Introduce your course of action, which is also known as your claim. State your reasons for supporting it.
- The second paragraph, or body, should provide logical reasons and relevant evidence supporting your claim that this course of action will help raise the standard of living. Use accurate, credible sources for your evidence.
- The third paragraph, or conclusion, should provide a statement that follows from and supports the argument you presented.

REVISE & EDIT

Read your draft to make sure that you make and support your claim with logical reasons and relevant evidence.

- Does the introduction get the attention of your audience and introduce your topic clearly?
- Does the body use words, phrases, and clauses that clarify the relationships among the claim, reasons, and evidence?
- Does your concluding statement follow from and support your argument?

Revise the draft to make sure you have established logical relationships among the claim, the reasons, and the evidence. Be sure you have presented your argument in a logical order. Then check your paper for errors in spelling and punctuation. Save your work.

PUBLISH & PRESENT

Now you are ready to publish and present your article. Add any images or graphs that enhance your ideas, and prepare a source list.

Then print out your article, or write a clean copy by hand. Post it in the classroom or to your class website.

Visual GLOSSARY

literacy rate

biodiversity

biodiversity *n.*, great variety of plants and animals

cost of living *n.*, the amount of money required to maintain a certain standard of living

diversified economy *n.*, an economy that produces a variety of products and services

ecotourism *n.*, travel to support a region's wildlife ecology and conservation efforts

income *n.*, the amount of money a person makes in a certain period of time

infant mortality rate *n.*, the number of infant deaths per 1,000 live births

life expectancy *n.*, the number of years that a person in a particular group or place can expect to live

literacy rate *n.*, the percentage of people who can read and write

malnutrition *n.*, a lack of nutrients needed to maintain health

overpopulation *n.*, a condition of having more people than an area can support

poverty line *n.*, the minimum income required to meet basic needs

standard of living *n.*, the level of available income, goods, and services

cost of living

standard of living

ecotourism

INDEX

SKILLS